OUR WORLD IN COLOUR

NEPAL

OUR WORLD IN COLOUR NEPAL

Photography by Bill Wassman
Text by Steve Van Beek

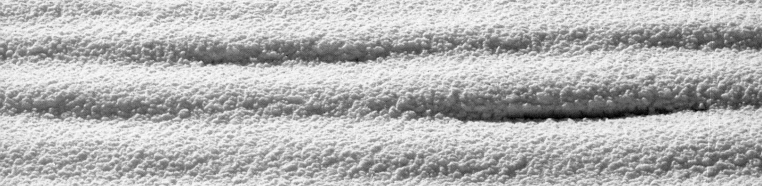

The Guidebook Company Limited

Distributors

Australia and New Zealand: The Book Company,
100 Old Pittwater Road, Brookvale, NSW 2100, Australia.

Canada: Prentice Hall Canada,
1870 Birchmount Road, Scarborough, Ontario MIP 257,
Canada.

Hong Kong: China Guides Distribution Services Ltd.,
14 Ground Floor, Lower Kai Yuen Lane, North Point, Hong Kong.

India and Nepal: UBS Publishers' Distributors Ltd.,
5 Ansari Road, Post Box 7015, New Delhi 110 002, India.

Singapore and Malaysia: MPH Distributors (S) PTE Ltd.,
601 Sims Drive, No. 03/07-21, Pan-I Complex, Singapore 1438.

UK: Springfield Books Limited,
Springfield House, Norman Road, Dendy Dale,
Huddersfield HD8 8TH, West Yorkshire, England.

USA: Publishers Group West Inc.,
4065 Hollis, Emeryville, CA 94608, USA.

Text and captions by Steve Van Beek

Photography by Bill Wassman. Additional
photographs by Magnus Bartlett (56 left, 58–9); Earl
Kowall (24–5 left/centre right, 30 top); Jeremy
Horner (17 bottom, 26, 62–3, 68, 72, 73, 74, 75);
Joanna Van Gruisen (16 top, 76).

Illustration by Mohan Lal Soni

Edited by Lesley Clark and Ralph Kiggell
An A to Z of Fun Facts by Mary Cooch

Designed by Joan Law Design & Photography
Cover colour separations by Sakai Lithocolour
Colour separations by Rainbow Graphic Arts Co., Ltd.
Printed in Hong Kong
by Toppan Printing Company (HK) Limited

ISBN 962-217-109-5

Title spread
*Trekking in Nepal, many people
rest at little mountain villages
such as this one — Ghaupokara
— which lies on the way to
Annapurna. The sloping roofs of
the houses help to prevent the
build up of snow, but here,
despite the intense glare of the
sun, the settled snow remains
crisp and sparkling.*

Right
*The gilded spire on the holy
stupa of Swayambhunath is
dominated by the hypnotic eyes
of Buddha. The third eye
symbolizes supreme wisdom
while the shepherd's-staff-like
'nose' beneath it is the Nepali
numeral 'one', and symbolizes
the unity of the people who
dwell in the Valley below.*

Pages 6–7
*In the fertile bowl of the
Kathmandu Valley many
different crops are grown. A
Newari farmer passes through
his mustard fields which have
ripened to a rich saffron yellow.
His daughter rests in one
basket, balanced by the mound
of vegetables in the other.*

Pages 8-9
*The Nepali New Year, held in
mid-April marks the first day of
the solar calendar. A boisterous
celebration, it allows the
release of energy pent up over a
year of toil, a magical day when
gods and demons dance. This
god-masked dancer whirls to
honour Mahakali, the Great
Goddess of Terror, before a
mural depicting her consort,
Bhairab, an avatar of Shiva in
his most frightening form. The
mural covers the wall of the
Chandeshwari Shrine near
Banepa just beyond the eastern
rim of Kathmandu Valley.*

Pages 10-11
*A cluster of colour as Tamangs,
one of the major tribes of
Nepal, gather in Kathmandu in
1975 for the coronation of King
Birendra. The gentle Tamangs
are Lama Buddhists from the
mountains beyond Kathmandu.
Their name suggests their
ancient role in the hierarchical
Himalayan society; in Tibetan,
Tamang means 'horse traders'.*

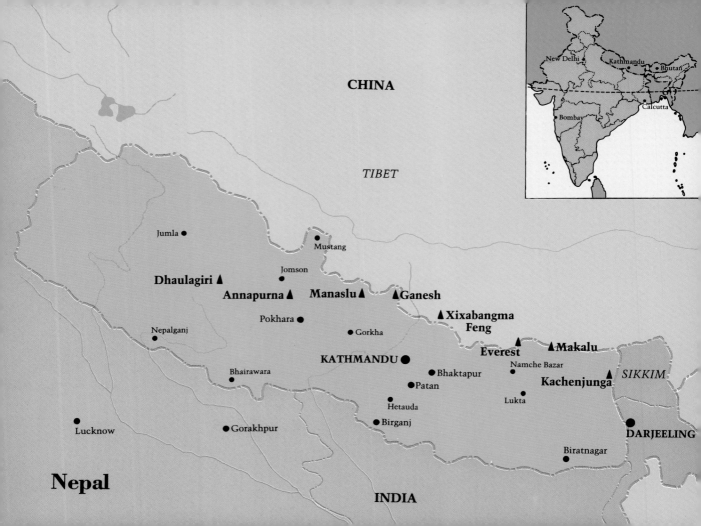

INTRODUCTION

IMAGINE A MASSIVE SHIP adrift in a raging cosmic storm. Helpless before the waves, it is forced closer and closer to the rocky shore, finally ploughing into it with such force that the leading edges of both ship and shore crunch together, each buckling skyward.

This fanciful description portrays the formation of the Himalaya, the product of a cataclysmic collision aeons ago between a gigantic floating continent and mainland Asia. It also explains the genesis of Nepal, a horizontal country pushed vertical, creating massifs of colossal heights beyond imagination. The souvenirs of its former incarnation beneath the sea are bound in loose rock at a height of 3,500 metres (12,000 feet). Today, walking through rocky scree, one often meets Tibetans offering to sell fossils of prehistoric marine creatures.

The Himalaya not only define the geography and history of this tiny Hindu Kingdom, they shape the very character and nature of its people and their indifferent, somewhat eccentric view of the world. Understand the mountains and you will understand Nepal and its development over the centuries.

Oblong and slightly larger than England, Greece or New Zealand, Nepal runs east and west along the spine of the Himalaya and contains eight of the ten highest peaks in the world. These mountains, including the formidable Mount Everest at 8,775 kilometres (29,028 feet), and dozens of smaller peaks, pierce a cobalt-blue sky. They hem in tiny valleys with inhabitants' houses dotted across the floors or clinging precariously to the mountains' steep flanks.

These daunting mountain barriers have walled out the world for centuries, ensuring Nepal's independence and preserving its culture more or less intact. Consequently, Nepal is a time capsule of a former age, its past embraced in its present like an ant in amber.

From the 13th to 18th centuries, the Kathmandu Valley was the domain of the Malla Dynasty who ruled aloof from political events south of the mountains. The outsiders who successfully breached the walls were not warriors but the vanguard of every peaceful invasion — the merchants and traders of Tibet, China, India and of the Mughal Empire.

A few would-be conquerors, like the Bengali Muslim sultan who destroyed Kathmandu's Swayambunath Temple in 1346, made it over the walls but few got further than the foothills. From the 14th century onwards, Indian Rajputs fleeing before the Muslim tide sweeping through India, sought refuge here. Independent fiefdoms in the valleys east and west of Kathmandu were established: it was these Rajputs who ultimately changed the political face of Nepal.

In the 19th century, British armies assailed the mountain walls but fell back. So impressed were they by Nepali courage, however, that they recruited Gurkha tribesmen with their famed curved knives, the *kukris*, to serve in crack British regiments. British officers, who have commanded them through two world wars and numerous skirmishes, rate them as the best soldiers in the world.

The mountains not only shut out the world, but separate Nepal into isolated kingdoms not unlike those of ancient Greece. These fiefdoms were finally united in 1768, when Prithvi Narayan Shah, monarch of the western kingdom of Gorkha, marched his armies along the mountain trails and occupied Kathmandu Valley. His chief accomplishment was to link his isolated subjects with a common language, Gorkhali, or, as it is known today, Nepali.

In 1816, wary of outside interference in its affairs, Nepal sealed its borders. In 1846, the Shah kings were usurped by their generals who established their own dynasty and these new quasi-monarchs, the Ranas, shut Nepal's gates even more firmly. Then, in 1951, in a unique switch from the normal mode of doing things — a shift which is typically Nepali — they replaced an oligarchy with a monarchy. King Tribhuvan regained control of his throne and, to public acclaim, returned the Shah

Limbu women of the middle hills of eastern Nepal. Like the Rais, Limbus are said to be descendants of the Kiratis, a fierce nomadic tribe that settled in Kathmandu Valley in the 7th century BC and were known as architects and craftsmen. When their empire fell, the remnants fled to the east, progenitors of the Limbu and Rai tribes whose men still fill the ranks of the famed Gurkha regiments.

Dynasty to power. Today, Nepal is the last Hindu monarchy in the world. King Tribhuvan's grandson, King Birendra, rules as a constitutional monarch. His government comprises a prime minister and his cabinet, and a parliament of representatives elected from *panchayats* (local councils) from each district of Nepal.

Surrounded by towering peaks, the Nepalis have created a culture that echoes these mountains. The valleys are filled with multi-tiered temples that draw the eye upwards, like the foothills and slopes of Macchapucchare and the Annapurnas. The *topis* (peaked hats) the men wear mimic the mountains. The Nepali flag, unique among the world's banners, looks like a pair of saw-toothed peaks laid on their sides. The towering stupas and Ashokan pillars; the shrines; the heaps of spices in the bazaar; the hillocks of white rice blanketed by *dahl; tarkari* on a brass dinner plate; the lilt of misty mountain music and the soaring voice of a singer or a two-stringed *sarangi*; even the serrated-ridge line of the Nepali language, all are inspired by the mountains. In short, the collective unconscious is a memory of mountains.

This is coupled with a proclivity to create uniquely Nepali ways of doing things: Nepal time is 5 hours 40 minutes ahead of GMT; Saturday is the weekly day off; and the men smoke their *bidis* (cigarettes) differently by shaping their fingers into a pipe.

Wedged between India and Chinese-ruled Tibet, Nepal's snowcapped peaks define its northern boundary like a white picket fence. This land-locked country is dependent upon the kindness of its neighbours for access to the outside world, its foreign policies are a balancing act. It takes special care not to offend India through which it must route 80 percent of its trade. For Nepal's people live under the roof of the world — Tibet — cut off from the ground, unable to reach it without permission from the downstairs' tenants — India.

With limited natural resources and a lack of the means to exploit or export them, Nepal is a poor country. Its years of isolation ensured its independence and cultural integrity but stunted its development. Today, it is largely an agrarian nation, self-sufficient in food terms with a little left over to export for the hard cash it needs to develop an industrial infrastructure and a strong public-service sector.

If Nepal's geography is a product of cataclysmic stress, its people are a direct antithesis, their equanimity and stoic natures are in diametric contrast to their surroundings. Their quiet demeanour reflects the sublime silence of the mountains, not the upheavals and earthquakes that periodically shake it to its core. Nor are they a despondent people; the first thing an outsider notices is the happy atmosphere. Walk along a mountain trail and hear a lilting flute or a farmer at work in his field, singing at the top of his voice, oblivious to an audience; singing for the sheer joy of it or as an anthem in praise of the gods.

Nepal's culture, like its mountains, seems to rise from the earth like a banyan tree tenaciously gripping the ground at a dozen points, its roots sunk deeply into it. Perhaps the people's affinity with the earth stems from the painfully short period they inhabit it. The mountains are hard taskmasters, exacting a toll for their beauty, forcing the Nepalis to scratch poor soil to eke out a living. The bitter cold of winter, the necessity of travelling long distances, the lack of communication, poor access to health care and an unbalanced diet, mean child mortality is high. One-fifth of the babies do not survive beyond the first few weeks of life, men live an average 44 years and women barely three years more. It is not a life of reflective thought but one of drudgery. People rise from the earth and, after a brief spell tilling the soil or toting heavy loads over mountain passes, they return to the earth again.

Nepal's 17 million people speak 36 languages and are divided into a dozen different ethnic groups spread over regions that run like bands across the length of Nepal. In the snowy north are the Buddhist Sherpas, renowned of Everest expeditions and mountain conquerors themselves. The middle regions hold the Rais, Limbus, Gurungs, Magars, Takhalis, Brahmans, Chettris, Tamangs and the Newars of the Kathmandu Valley. The jungles at the foothills of the Himalaya are home to the hardy Tharus and the torrid Terai is inhabited by a people indistinguishable from northern Indians. In all, it is a cultural mix of surprising diversity for a country so small.

This heterogeneity is reflected in the religions the Nepalis embrace. Buddhism, Hinduism and Islam flourish in harmony with one another. Buddhist stupas and Hindu temples coexist on the Kathmandu Valley floor; Hindu shrines and Moslem mosques share the towns of the Terai.

Buddhism and Hinduism, in contrast to the austere Islam, give colour and dimension to Nepali life. The muted shades of native dress and the temples are counterpoised by the brass of plaques, the gleam of gold images, crimson and mustard-yellow cloth, orange marigold blossoms and scarlet hibiscus and incense sticks that decorate the shrines in cities and along the mountain tracks. The fragrance of sandalwood incense smoke and the scent of melted wax from hundreds of candles ablaze at a shrine perfume the air. Sonorous Tibetan chants, shuddering alpenhorns, resonant gongs and tinkling temple bells delight the ears.

Hinduism is not a quiet religion but one of singing and dancing in celebration of a god or goddess. The great pantheon of gods in the Hindu hierarchy give the normally quiet Nepalis ample opportunity to vent their high spirits. Nearly every day, Nepal echoes with the sounds of a new festival or ceremony. Diwali, with its thousands of candles; Dasain, with its animal sacrifices; Holi, and dozens of other festivals swirl around the visitor. They give a glimpse of the inner lives of Nepalis, normally hidden behind the walls of their sombre selves.

Nepal has intrigued outsiders for centuries. Fablers sang of lost horizons and of Shangri-la; Nepal met all the criteria. It was exotic, otherworldly, unique. Although the doors finally opened a crack in 1951, it was only in 1953 that the rest of the world began to know more about Nepal. That year, a Sherpa, Tenzing Norgay and a New Zealander, Sir Edmund Hillary, became the first men in history to climb to the summit of Mount Everest.

Despite Nepal's new notoriety, few travellers ventured into the land; it was just too far away and the means of reaching it were too uncertain. There were no airfields and not until 1956 was the first road carved along the steep mountain faces and across the Kathmandu Valley floor. For all but monied travellers, entering Nepal meant trekking to it or riding buses over bone-crunching roads on a nine-hour journey around hairpin bends.

The late '60s, the era of the Flower Children, saw the first influx of Western travellers in significant numbers. They flowed into the Valley and, from there, along the trekking trails that led to Everest and the Jomosom region above the western town of Pokhara. Soon, they were arriving in torrents. Today, Nepal is struggling to accommodate these foreign tourists with its limited resources.

In a land where only a generation ago few foreigners would be seen, the Nepali response to this flood of strangers is odd. Aside from the attention showered on them by children and beggars, visitors are virtually ignored, unless they request help; a refreshing departure indeed from the receptions received in many other countries. Here, the tourist is an observer, able to watch daily life without altering it.

The epicentre of Nepal, if such a word can be used in a country so threatened by earth tremors, is Kathmandu Valley. It is a bowl cupped by a ridge of mountains which ancient legend claims was once a lake whose waters gushed out when the god Manjushri cut a notch in the wall with his mighty sword. Geologists offer the more prosaic explanation that an earthquake or other natural disaster breached the rim of the bowl, allowing the waters to drain into the plains to the south.

On an autumn day, travel to the hill west of Kathmandu crowned by Swayambunath, the magnificent stupa whose Buddha's eyes are ever open, keeping watch over the city. From here, the Valley spreads out at one's feet. The towns, like islands of buff-brown houses, in seas of lush green rice shoots and sulphur-yellow mustard

Gods in modern and ancient guise. The welcoming hands of a beneficent guardian dominate a poster decorating a Kathmandu wall. The fierce mien of Sa-dag, Tibetan God of the Earth, is painted on a stucco wall near Swayambhunath.

The monal pheasant is a high mountain dweller and serves as Nepal's national bird. It is also known as the danphe *or 'bird of nine colours'.*

Rama and Sita, the epitome of steadfast love. The story has struck a resonant chord in Asian hearts, for centuries providing the principal theme of drama and dance in the countries of South and Southeast Asia. This stone depiction is found in a Bhaktapur temple.

blossoms rest under an azure sky. And always, the white mountain peaks provide a stunning backdrop to life in the Valley.

The four cities of Kathmandu, Patan, Bhaktapur and Kirtipur once contended for dominion over the Valley. Kathmandu was victorious. When Prithvi Narayan Shah invaded in 1768, in his quest to unify Nepal, he chose this ancient city as his capital.

Kathmandu, named for the *Kasthamandap* ('house of wood') which stands at its centre, now has a population of 300,000. It is a city of mystical aura, with monuments and gods at every turning. For centuries, it developed at its own pace and, even in the '60s, seemed locked in another age, a relic of a medieval past. Wags commented that Nepal was rushing headlong from the 12th to the 13th century. Visitors likened its streets to a film set from Fielding's *Tom Jones*. Such comments were not made in derision but in awe and appreciation of a people that had maintained their rich culture with full confidence in its integrity, rather than rushed blindly after the gewgaws of the West. What it had adopted from the West had been of its own choosing. The princes bought Rolls Royces but did not build roads over the mountains for that would bring unwanted foreign intrusion. Instead, their cars were simply dismantled in the Terai and carried into the Valley where they were reassembled for the city's crude roadways and lanes.

But today, the lure of Westernization is too strong for Nepal to resist and much has changed. It now has television. Jetliners disgorge visitors by the thousands and the trekking trails are experiencing traffic jams. Even the inviolate rivers now cushion rubber rafts with terrified riders experiencing spray and adrenaline rushes as they hurtle down whitewater that is more white than water!

Yet, Nepal is resilient. It can withstand the onslaughts of the outside world for some time yet. Evidence of that is found in Kathmandu itself which has been hardest hit by the avalanche of visitors. Changes have taken place but they are cosmetic changes; the core remains unaltered. Whereas the cultural elements of many Asian cities have survived as tiny pockets lost amidst skyscrapers, in Kathmandu they remain the dominant feature on the landscape.

Kathmandu is a city of dusty red brick, carved wooden sills, and dark roof tiles. Its colours suggest sobriety, yet the city glows, suffused with the resonance and redolence of its busy daily life. Contrasts to the squat, three-storey shop-houses are provided by the temples and the old Rana palaces of the city's former rulers. The largest, Singhadurbar, once contained 1,700 rooms, making it the biggest single-family residence in the world. With the return of the Shah Dynasty, it became the National Secretariat but, unfortunately, much of it burned down in a disastrous fire in 1973. Other Rana palaces survive, however, many of them enjoying second incarnations as hotels!

Kathmandu proper is defined on the east by the broad parade ground called the Tundikhel, and on the west and south by the Vishnumati and Bagmati rivers. Beyond the walls of the modern concrete buildings that line New Road, is the core of the city — the durbar square — anchored by the Kasthamandap that gave the city its name. Here, Hanuman Dhoka, the former royal palace with roofs representing each of the four key cities of the Valley, and the other major temples cluster.

In the narrow lanes leading off from the durbar square lives the real Kathmandu. Cutting at an oblique angle through the heart of the old city is the lane leading northeast to Asantole and beyond. It was once the main trade route to Tibet and typifies not only Kathmandu, but also many other towns of Nepal. It meanders between three-storey brick buildings whose front stoops serve as display counters for the wares that tumble out of the shops. Pungent smells of yellow cumin, red chillies, cinnamon, curry powder and mustard seed assail one's nostrils. A grey Brahmin cow wanders from shop to shop, nibbling a bit of vegetable here, a bit of rice there but soon discovers that its divinity under Hinduism does not protect it from a sharp whack on its flanks by an irate vendor.

The upper windows of the houses are of gorgeously carved wood latticework that glows in the late afternoon sun pouring down the street, bathing everything in its warm light. Many of the open windows are set at a slant to overlook the street; women and children have an excellent view of the stage below them from the box seats thus created. With kohl-lined eyes, they gaze down on the throng, giggling and commenting on the passing scene. From some windows, intricately patterned, hand-woven Tibetan carpets are hung to air or to sell. From the eaves, garlic, corn or red chillies strung like Chinese firecrackers are suspended to dry for winter use.

The street itself is a tumult, passers-by are compressed by the closeness of the lane into a flowing river of humanity. A bicycle rider, bravely ringing his bell, weaves and brakes and then shoots through a gap which opens momentarily, nimbly ma-noeuvring past spice sellers and piles of bright aluminium kitchen pots. Sari-clad women with gold-encased turquoise studding their ears, crimson henna streaking down the partings of their ebon hair and scarlet hems encircling their black saris, hug shiny brass pots as they trudge barefooted to a fountain. And always, the men's topis bob up and down, looking from a distance like an avalanche of tiny mountains rolling down a hillside.

The houses enclose courtyards with wells or Hindu shrines at their centre. Just as you cross a narrow pass to enter Kathmandu Valley, you slip through a narrow door to enter these hidden courtyards away from the cacophony of the street outside. These courtyards connect with one another by open doorways to create an enormous maze — a separate city in itself. In neighbouring Patan, it is possible to travel half a kilometre across town from one courtyard to another, passing through a lush meadow with grazing cows completely enclosed by brick houses, and on through more court-yards to arrive at a distant district.

As in all major Valley towns, Kathmandu's chief inhabitants are the Newars. No one is quite sure where they came from; some historians suggest they originated in Gujarat, near Bombay. They speak their own language and observe a form of Bud-dhism and it is their culture more than any other that one sees in Kathmandu. They built nearly all the temples that greeted Prithvi Narayan Shah's eyes when he stood on the Valley wall and surveyed what would soon become his realm.

Like the Mongols in China, and other victors who were converted by the van-quished, the Gurkha invaders bowed before the monuments of Newari culture. Eventually, they found their own creative voice which was an amalgam dominated by Newari artistic ideals and a radical departure from that of the area from which they had come.

It is easier to appreciate Newari culture in pure form in other cities of the Valley. There, the past has been better preserved and fewer institutions have been altered to cater to visitors. Patan, west of the Bagmati River, is fabled as the town of a thousand golden roofs but is best known as a city of craftsmen. One-third the size of Kath-mandu, it is bounded by four stupas said to have been built by the Indian Emperor Ashoka who converted much of northern India to Buddhism in the third century BC. Patan displays an adherence to India in other respects as well. At its heart lies a durbar square embracing a temple of South Indian design.

Bhaktapur is the third city of the triumvirate that once ruled the Valley. Located to the east at the end of the city tram line, it has perhaps the most Newari influence with 90 percent of the population from this ethnic group. Its efforts to retain its past is evidenced by restoration work recently completed in its town square. There, the inhabitants were moved out temporarily, their houses returned to their original mint condition, then the residents were moved back in. The result is a living museum, the past preserved *in situ*.

Kirtipur, in the southeast corner of the Valley, was never a great power but its appeal lies both in its setting and in the fact that today it is virtually ignored by visitors. It runs along the spine of Siamese-twin hills, a defence that did not prevent

Closely akin to the Limbu, the Rai are descendants of the Kiratis and also inhabit the eastern portion of the middle Himalaya.

The Himalayan range containing Mount Everest forms a backdrop for a Sherpa house high in the Khumbu Valley near Lukla. For decades, the Valley and the airport at Lukla have been the staging points for assaults on Everest, Lhotse and Cho Oyu, three of the world's seven highest peaks.

its being overrun in the 18th century. Prithvi Narayan Shah was so incensed at its defender's intransigence and their thumbing their noses at him that he ordered that those noses and the lips of all males except wind musicians be cut off! Because of its isolation, Kirtipur, more than any other city of the Valley, continues to live in the past, giving the visitor a glimpse of town life a century ago.

If the Kathmandu Valley is somewhat removed from the mainstream of Asian life, Nepal's mountain villages are even more so. As little as two decades ago, they were completely isolated, accessible only by walking for days over the mountains. The first wheels many villagers saw were those on an aeroplane, not on a bullock cart. Today, 3,000 kilometres (1,864 miles) of road has been scratched across the country, most of it linking cities of the Terai. There are 40 airfields that help connect the main population centres.

Pre-dating Hinduism and Buddhism is jhankrism or shamanism. While jhankrism has survived in the hills as a separate practice, in the Kathmandu Valley, certain elements have blended with Hindu and Buddhist rites. The three religions observe the same rites and practice at the same temples. The shamans enter trances to drive away the spirits of sickness and death and perform rites to ensure bountiful harvests. During Mela, they don peacock feather headdresses and flowing white robes and beat drums as they whirl around the temple courtyard to dance themselves into trances.

In the far north are the Sherpa and Bhotia villages with their yaks, *tsampa* (barley meal), buttered tea, Buddhist stupas, cairns and tales of fierce 'yetis', the so-called abominable snowmen who dine on lost mountaineers.

Of the lower valley towns, Pokhara in the west is the most important. Set in the foothills of the Annapurnas, its architecture is typical of that of most mountain towns. Houses are built of stone cemented together with mud and covered with yet more mud. The lower portions of the houses are daubed to waist height in ochre paint and the upper portions in white paint. Roofs may be made of slate, wood or thatch. Streets are paved with large slabs of stone against which the iron-shod hooves of tiny mules click as they carry their heavy loads of rice and salt into remote villages higher in the hills.

The road linking Kathmandu with India is called the Rajpath and ranks as one of the most hair-raising rides known. Completed in 1956, it twists and turns along the cliff faces as it makes its gradual descent. So steep are some of the hillsides that at one point, you look down and see a tiny bus on the opposite hill 25 kilometres (15 miles) away! The unpaved road is plied by huge trucks and buses which occasionally meet head-on. The drivers manoeuvre carefully to edge past each other; the passengers on the outside lane see no road beside them, just a bottomless chasm.

At Hetaunda and Simra, the Rajpath intersects with the East-West Highway, which travels through jungle and plains as it slices the country in half. The rainforests here contain several animal reserves, and are inhabited by the hardy Tharus who are said to have developed a resistance to the malaria that infests this pestilential region.

Books tend to give the Terai short shrift in their descriptions of Nepal and the observer, having raised his eyes to the mountains, often overlooks what lies at his feet. Yet this is not only Nepal's most important region, it is its future.

The hill region, with its inhospitable climate and rocky soil cannot feed itself and must depend upon the farmers of the Terai. With its richer soil and its year-round sunshine, the Terai is Nepal's chapatti-basket. It produces not only the rice the rest of the country eats but the exports which earn the country vital foreign revenue.

But it is hard to love the Terai. This is not the romantic land of jungles, tigers and rhinos, the Terai of Chitwan with its lush rainforests. It is a skillet on the Gangetic Plains where the summertime temperatures can exceed 46°C (115°F). Ranging from 25–40 kilometres (15–25 miles) wide, it is flat and featureless, lying barely 100 metres (328 foot) above sea level.

Its people are Indian, their allegiances uncertain. Having more in common with India, they stand with their backs to the mountains, looking southward. Tell any Nepali outside the Valley that you are going to Kathmandu and he will say 'Ah, you are going to Nepal.' Here in the Terai, it takes on a special meaning, it reveals the traditional antipathy between mountain and plains people.

The Terai's most important contribution to the world occurred in the small town of Lumbini in the sixth century BC. There, a prince of the Sakya clan was born who was destined to change the lives of millions of people. Known as Gautama Buddha, his influence spread far beyond Nepal's borders, to the very ends of Asia and beyond.

Although known as an agricultural region, the Terai is also the cradle of Nepal's industrial development. Its centre is at the southeastern city of Biratnagar but that future is also being built in the central town of Birgunj and the western town of Bhaiwara. With their access to railheads, raw materials and power, they are Nepal's cities of the 21st century.

Twentieth-century Nepal has become an easy country to discover. One can hop around by aeroplane or trek through some of the most beautiful scenery known. But there is an even easier way to experience the country, and it doesn't require walking at all! Simply sit on the upper ledge of a temple in the heart of Kathmandu or lean on the brick wall around a public bathing pond. Wait there long enough, and Nepal will come to you. Few cities offer so many sensorial stimuli at a single imbibing as Kathmandu does. Stay in one spot for one day and glimpse the whole of Nepal.

Yet this is only the beginning, to taste this nectar is to become addicted. One is compelled to delve deeper into the heart of the country, to sink into the Nepali cultural fabric and enwrap oneself in its folds. So sensuous is this experience, that it is hard to leave the country, and one envies the meditators and sadhus embraced within its walls forever, entranced by Nepal — a splendid world within a pinpoint.

The colourful gateway that leads to Bodhnath. A sister stupa to Swayambhunath, it lies an equal distance to the east of Kathmandu, directly in line with the old royal palace and the hilltop Swayambhu.

Midway between the antique buildings of Kathmandu and the modern concrete structures are these shops whose owners occupy the upper floors. The buildings share with the old style the three-storey height, the shop doors that fold open to become display cases for goods, and the tall windows that open like French doors.

Following pages
Nama Buddha, 'Name of the Buddha', hums with hosannas as the winds set the prayer flags flapping, wafting ancient scriptures skyward to bring blessings. The shrine sits atop a small hill at Namara, one valley east of Kathmandu.

Left
It is generally believed that Patan's four Ashok stupas were built by the great Buddhist emperor Ashoka himself. This stupa lies to the north of central Patan, the remaining three are sited to the east, west and south. The most spectacular of the four, it can be easily recognized by its great white dome and yellow pinnacle which rise up over the cluster of rooftops surrounding it.

Above
A monsoon storm brews over Patan, the second of the triumvirate of cities that once ruled Kathmandu Valley. Across the Bagmati River to the south of Kathmandu, Patan is known as 'the city of a thousand golden roofs'. Called Lalitpur or 'Beautiful City' by its inhabitants, it is famed for its craftsmen and woodcarvers whose art decorates the elaborate windows and doors of its palaces and temples.

Top
The woodcarvers' art is evident in the windows of Patan Palace. Its terraces provide a stage for play and daily activities under the watchful gaze of twin sentinels.

Centre
Hanuman Dhoka, 'Gate of the Albino Monkey God Hanuman' of the Ramayana epic, was once the royal palace. Wrapped in red cloth, the god is shaded by an umbrella decorated with the Nepali flag depicting the sun and the moon.

Above
Each of the three main cities of Kathmandu Valley has a durbar square, or palace plaza. Kathmandu's durbar square is dominated by the Shiva Temple on the left. Hidden in the shadows under the eaves of the Shiva-Parvati Temple on the right are wooden statues of the amorous couple looking down from an upper window onto the passing crowds.

Left
*Women hug their shawls
around them, perhaps against
the chill morning air, perhaps
in anticipation of wresting a
bargain from a market vendor.*

Right
*A stone Ganesh, the elephant
god, is streaked with henna
powder by Hindu faithful. The
elephant-headed son of Shiva
and Parvati, Ganesh is revered
as the remover of obstacles and
the bestower of good fortune.*

Left
The city of Kathmandu sees great contrasts of wealth and poverty, drabness and gaiety, with the royal family of Nepal providing much of the pomp and circumstance. The Royal Calvalry turn out magnificently — all plumes and shining buckles — for one of the many annual royal processions for their king, reputed to be the seventh richest man in the world.

Above
Meanwhile, a peerer of the realm surveys the street from one of the many ancient cars that cruise through Kathmandu's streets.

Right
While not so colourful, this regiment seem equally proud of their country as they prepare to salute the king during the Indrajatra festival, one of the most spectacular occasions in the Nepali year.

Above
Durbar Square in Patan is the focal point of religious, royal, commercial and communal life. The palace on the right and the clustered temples opposite it serve as display counters for wares. They are also gathering places for business and social meetings, the tiered ledges serving as convenient seats for the weary.

Left
The Krishna Temple is one of two in Patan's Durbar Square that honours the mischievous boy who grew to become one of the favourite gods of the Hindu hierarchy of deities. The octagonal temple dedicated to the blue-skinned god with the crescent moon in his hair, is built of stone.

Right
Sadhus (holy men) and citizens take refuge from torrential rain under the eaves of the royal palace in Patan's Durbar Square.

Left
Crowning thin poles, these banners, flags and branches carry the devotional prayers of Tibetan Buddhists; their bleak silhouettes seem to emphasize the powerful solitude of this remote mountain region near Helambu.

Right
Monks of the Gelupa — the yellow-hat sect — move solemnly towards the Bodhnath Stupa, the largest stupa in Nepal, during Tibetan New Year celebrations. Indian, Nepali, Ladakhi and Tibetan Buddhists gather once a year for the event.

Above
The Rato Machhendranath Temple in
Patan houses the extraordinary red
Machhendranath mask — the face of the
god worshipped by Buddhists as an aspect
of the benevolent god Avalokitesvara, and
by Hindus as Shiva, the bringer of rain and
fertility. Once a year, the mask is
'disembodied' and placed in a great
chariot which forms the central part of a
huge religious procession through Patan.

Right
The snout and fangs of a fierce temple
guardian remain shiny where countless
pilgrims — partly in awe, partly in mock
defiance — have repeatedly rubbed them.
These same pilgrims rub the ubiquitous
red tikka paste that on other wooden and
bronze statuary has obscured the fine
carving. This griffon-like figure stands
sentinel at the Kwa Bahal in Patan.

Left
The all-seeing eyes of Buddha peer from pure gold in four directions. The plaque on his forehead commemorates the Buddha in various positions of meditation while the 13 tiered disks rising like a crown represent the 13 degrees of knowledge, the stairsteps to nirvana, symbolized by the parasol at their summit.

Above
Legend says that Kathmandu Valley was a gigantic lake until the god Manjushri wished to take a closer look at a beautiful lotus growing at its centre. He smote the Valley wall with his sword at Chobar and allowed the waters to drain into the Gangetic Plains. A more prosaic explanation blames an earthquake but Manjushri continues to be regarded as the patriarch god of the Valley and is depicted in bronze statues with his sword raised or in murals as in this one at Swayambhunath Temple.

Above
Rising from the base of the hills on which Swayambhunath rests is a flagstone stairway that rises gently and then arcs into a steep ascent that taxes even the physically fit. The path is marked by three Buddhas and dozens of small stupas.

Right
Looming in the early morning mists on the slopes of Swayambhu are mani *(prayer stones) in Tibetan script daubed with brightly coloured powder and spelling out powerful incantations.*

Vishnu the Preserver, one of the all-powerful trinity of deities that
guide the universe's destiny. Legend says that among his
thousands of incarnations is that of the god Narayan. Lying on the
cosmic ocean, Narayan slept deeply and a lotus grew from his
naval. The lotus bloomed to reveal Brahma the Creator, another of
the trinity, who then turned to the task of forming the world. On a
plateau above the Valley, at a place called Budhanilkantha
Budhana, a stone Vishnu recalling the myth of creation is an
object of veneration by all Nepali Hindus.

Above
The ubiquitous lingam *is generally associated with the god Shiva. The phallic pestle is a symbol of potency while the* yoni *or mortar in which it stands represents the female element. Together they symbolize passion and the force of creation in the universe. This Shiva lingam is at the holy city of Pashupatinath.*

Left

Pashupatinath, on the banks of the Bagmati River, is one of Hinduism's holiest sites. It is dedicated to Shiva, who embraces the dual concepts of creation and destruction, and thus represents the transition between the end of one existence and the beginning of a new one. Hindus come here to spend their final days on earth. This sacred and private place is closed to all but Hindus.

Above

A poster of Shiva, recognized by his trident, suggests his dual nature and the inevitability of transition from one form to another. Although regarded as a god of death and destruction, his serene smile signifies calm acceptance of the nature of all things: to shed one existence by dying and acquire a new one through rebirth.

Right

A stone Buddha, carved on a stele and said to date from the sixth century gazes towards Pashupatinath across the Bagmati River.

Left
During Tibetan New Year celebrations, held around February every year, great processions of lamas follow the portrait of the Dalai Lama to the Bodhnath Stupa in Patan. Later, pilgrims, who have gathered from all over the Himalaya, watch masked dancers enact demon-chasing dramas that will ensure good luck and prosperity for the coming year.

Above
After spinning gracefully around the refined setting of the Mul Chowk courtyard in Patan, a Kathak dancer — gorgeously dressed in flowing skirts and scarves, and arrayed with fresh garlands of yellow marigolds — whirls to a dramatic halt. The drummer, discreetly positioned in the shadows, beats out the rhythm to which her feet exactly correspond.

Above
A sadhu or Hindu holy man in a pool swimming in marigolds at Pashupatinath, holds aloft a sacred sword in a symbolic rite to honour a god.

Left
Few Hindu statues are left unadorned by devotees. This one at Bhaktapur, of Krishna amidst the cowgirls, has been daubed in red paste by worshippers who arrive each morning to smooth on colour with their fingers and leave blossoms at its base to honour the god.

Above
A sadhu sings at Pashupatinath. Normally of the Brahmanic caste, sadhus are ascetics who live as wandering mendicants, depending on the largess of the devout for their food and sleeping nights in small groups in copses outside villages. They daub themselves with ash, mat their hair — which they never cut nor wash — and spend their days in meditation or chanting, often in a marijuana-induced fog.

Right
A stone statue of Buddha with the green patina of age and misty mountains, and the bright colours applied by the faithful to pay respect to him.

*Dusk casts an orange glow on the white
flanks of the Bodhnath stupa. The white
base of the stupa represents the four
elements: earth, air, fire, and water, of
which the cosmos is composed.*

Top
Prayer flags tied from the parasol to the balustrade flutter and flap, lips that whisper prayers into the wind sweeping across the Valley on its way to the high mountains, carrying chants·with it.

Centre
A Buddhist lama blows a brass double-reed horn at a ceremony at Bodhnath stupa.

Above
Myth says that Bodhnath, the largest stupa in Nepal, was built by a poor but frugal widow named Kangma. When she had enough money to erect a monument, she inveigled the king to give her a piece of land equal in size to that which could be covered by a buffalo hide. The shrewd lady cut the skin into narrow strips to form a border around a huge plot of land on which she built her stupa.

Left
Nyatapola, Nepal's largest and the most impressive of Bhaktapur temples, is guarded by five pairs of mythical creatures, each pair said to be ten times more powerful than the pair immediately above it. It is dedicated to the goddess Siddhi Lakshmi, a Tantric deity, whose various avatars are depicted on the 108 struts that hold up the roof, 108 being considered an auspicious number in Hinduism and Buddhism.

Above
Bhaktapur contains the largest percentage of Newaris, the dominant ethnic group of the Kathmandu Valley. The women can be recognized by the red bands at the hems of their ebon saris.

Above
Strings of chillies like firecrackers at Chinese New Year are suspended from the windows to dry. This is a common sight throughout Nepal during the months of September and October.

Right
Chillies are dried on straw mats in Bhaktapur's Dattatraya Square. The square was the heart of the original town of Bhaktapur and is dominated by the Dattatraya Temple with twin Malla wrestlers guarding its portals.

Above
Marking the entrance to the Harisiddhi Temple in the eastern Valley town of Banepa is a torana *(a carved and gilded plaque) depicting the god the temple enshrines. The god, Vishnu, is protected by his vehicle, the garuda, who clasps in his claws his arch-enemies, the nagas or serpents.*

Left
A poster on a Pashupati wall advertises a popular brand of bidi, *the tiny, harsh-tasting cigars that are all wrapper and no tobacco.*

Above
A pensive Tibetan woman reflects on ethereal things or nothing at all as she leans on a balustrade holding Tibetan prayer wheels.

Right
A scarlet dakini *or god of death with its necklace of skulls at a Newari temple in Kathmandu Valley.*

Following pages
The Annapurna Range from a village high in the Pokhara Valley. On the left is its most picturesque peak, Macchapacchare.

Right
Chetri women weed rice paddies in Kathmandu Valley. Chetri defines a caste ranking directly below Brahman but in Nepal the distinction between ranks is hazed to a greater extent than in India. Once occupying high positions in the royal courts, Chetris originated in the middle hills of western Nepal and now spend their lives as farmers and tradespeople.

Following pages
The placid blue waters of Phewa Tal just outside Pokhara reflect the beauty of the Annapurnas.

Above
Mountain slopes and streams provide a plentiful supply of stones which can be cemented together with mud to make sturdy houses. Out-buildings are often loosely constructed of slabs of logs.

Left
A Sherpani or female Sherpa. The Buddhist Sherpas, high-mountain dwellers acclimatized to thin air and a harsh life, make excellent mountaineers. The men and women both toil to carry heavy loads up slopes that would destroy most walkers.

Above
A market in an eastern Nepal hill town under the canopy of a pipul tree, its roots providing resting places and display shelves for rice and other agricultural produce.

Right
A Rai cultivator of eastern Nepal follows a plough pulled by a pair of bullocks.

Following pages
Moonlight and mountain peaks, themselves unworldly beyond description, known only to those who have trespassed in them and known their silence and pristine beauty.

Left
Kagbeni at an elevation of 4,000 meters (1,219 feet), has sparse vegetation and fewer trees and resembles a village on the moon. The men have traditionally traded with Tibet but retreat to Pokhara Valley before the icy winds that knife down the passes in the winter.

Right
In remote mountain villages, such as Kagbeni, and elsewhere in Nepal, there is little organized schooling for children; this little Manangi girl will help her parents with their daily chores and learn the skills she will use for the rest of her life.

Preceding pages
Winter in Manang Valley behind the white wall of the Annapurnas. Manangis live in four-storey stone houses which are stepped so that the roof of one serves as the terrace of the floor above. Manangis are famed as traders, their business taking them far beyond the borders of Nepal, to Asian cities like Hong Kong and Singapore.

Above
The jagged Khumbu Range which divides Nepal from Tibet has as its centrepiece Sagarmatha, 'The Brow of the Oceans'. It is better known in the West as Mount Everest, named after 19th-century British surveyor-general, George Everest.

Right
Ganesh Himal rises out of the mists covering the floor of Kathmandu Valley.

Above
Makalu, the world's fifth-highest mountain, seems a minor member of the Himalaya when compared with its close neighbours, Lhotse and Everest.

Left
Thatched stilt huts are the typical dwellings of the Thakuri people. The space below the hut provides a useful area for keeping livestock, and storing grain and farming utensils.

Above
Bells to be rung to alert the gods to attend to a supplicant's prayers at Kalinchoke.

Right
Chorten (Tibetan stupas) are common sights along ridges and at passes and notches in mountain ranges. Travellers carry stones from the valleys below and place them here as a benediction to the mountains. Many are carved with Tibetan Buddhist incantations, the most common being Om Mane Padme Om.

Left
*Ama Dablan may be outranked by nearby
Everest but its crystal-shaped peak is more
memorable.*

Above
*Blushing in the dusk sky, jagged peaks in
the Khumbu region, their surfaces tortured
like glacial ice, rise above Gokyo Valley.*

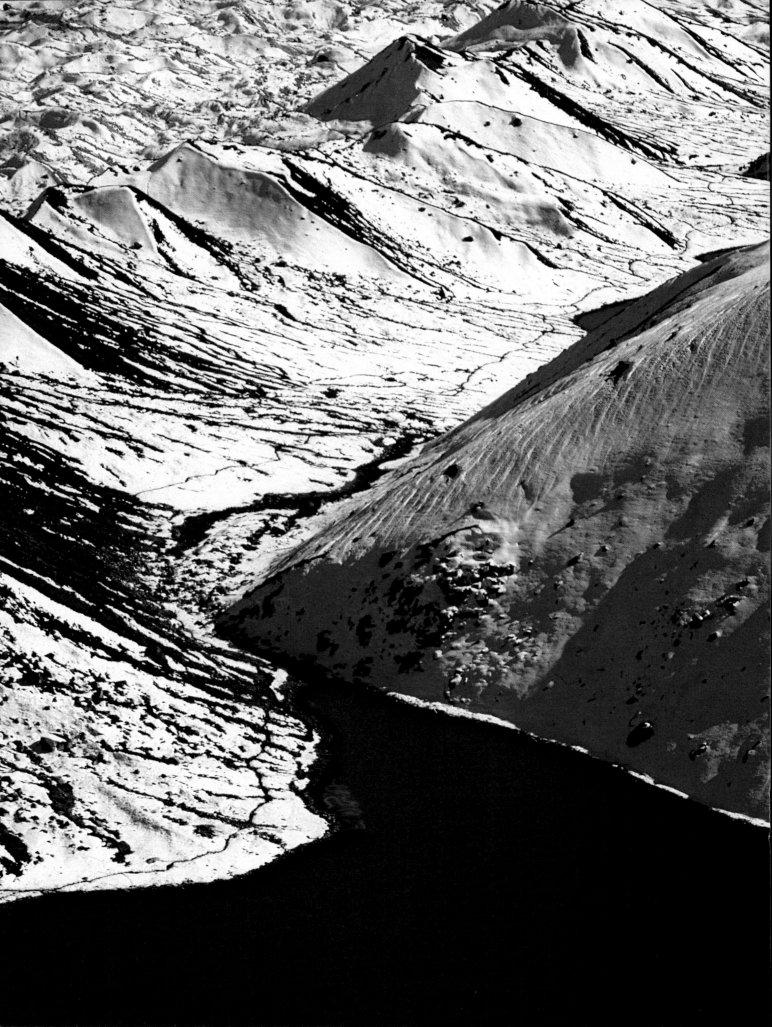

Left
*The downy coat of winter clads
mountains surrounding Gokyo
Lake in the Sagarmatha
National Park.*

Right
Rara Lake

Above
Summer in the hills with their grazing yaks and crimson-robed Buddhist monks, is depicted in this Sherpa mural on the walls of the most famous gompa *or monastery in the Everest region.*

Right
Muktinath Valley, on the trail to the forbidden kingdom of Mustang and Tibet beyond, receives the first snows of winter.

Following pages
The mist-shrouded Chandragiri, 'The Mountain of the Moon', stands like a watchtower on the Valley wall. It looms over Thankot, key town on the Rajpath Highway and gateway from the Gangetic Plains to the south.

AN A TO Z OF FUN FACTS

A

Area 145,391 km² (56,139 mi²).

Arniko A Newari architect and master craftsman who, in the late 13th century, was invited to Tibet to build important stupas and cast historic images. His fame reached the court of the Ming emperor of China and he was invited to join the court as the 'controller of the imperial manufactures'. The multi-tiered dagoba style buildings of China and Japan owe their origin to this appointment. Arniko is one of many Newari craftsmen who have influenced the art and architecture of the east. The modern highway from Kathmandu to the Chinese–Tibetan border is appropriately named after him.

B

Buddha This literally means 'the Enlightened One' and was the name given to the founder of Buddhism, Siddhartha Gautama, who was born in Lumbini, Nepal in about 543 BC. He taught that suffering is caused by attachment to people and things of the world and can be overcome by freeing the self of the desire for these things. This is achieved by the Eightfold Path of right views, right intent, right speech, right conduct, right livelihood, right effort, right mindfulness and right meditation.

Budhanilkantha A famous image of the god Vishnu appears to float in a lake at Budhanilkantha. The representation is carved out of a block of stone and shows Vishnu reclining on a bed of snakes. In November every year thousands of people gather to pay homage to Vishnu at this site and cover the image in flowers. However, it is said that if the King looks at this image he will be cursed.

C

Capital Kathmandu (population 300,000).

Climate The monsoon season lasts from June to October. In the low lying regions summer is tropical and humid, but the months of December and January are cold.

Currency Nepali rupee.

D

Dzu-tch According to the Sherpas, the dzu-tch is a type of yeti which is about eight feet tall and likes to eat cattle. It is one of three types of yeti which reputedly inhabit the Himalaya region of Nepal.

E

Ethnic groups Tribal groups include Gurung, Limbu, Magar, Newar, Rai, Sherpa, the Brahmins and Chhetris. A large number of Indians and some 12,000 Tibetans also make their home in Nepal.

F

Flag Nepal's national flag is triangular which makes Nepal the only country in the world which does not have a rectangular flag.

G

Geography Nepal is a land of extreme geographical features. 25% of the country is more than 3,000 m (10,000 ft) above sea level. 20% is less than 300 m (1,000 ft) above sea level. Three latitudinal mountain ranges extend across the country. In the south the Churia and Siwalik ranges rise steeply from the Gangetic Plain. In the north the Great Himalayan range forms a barrier of perpetual ice and snow. Three river systems cross the country vertically — the Karnali, Gandaki and Kosi. However, the latitude of Kathmandu is about the same as Florida and Kuwait and slightly south of New Delhi.

Government The form of government in Nepal is based on the Panchayat Constitution of 1962 which set up a two-tiered system of administration. At national level the government consists of HM the King, the Palace Secretariat, the Council of Ministers, the Ministerial Secretariat, the National Panchayat and thirteen Ministries and their departments. At the local level elected councils share responsibility with government ministers for implementing policy decisions.

Gurkhas The original Gurkha troops were Gorkhalis from Gorkha, the small principality in central Nepal, from which Prithvi Narayan Shah had conquered the Kathmandu Valley in 1768 and unified Nepal. Gurkha troops are composed mainly of Thakuri, Magar and Gurung men. The first regular Gorkhali battalions were formed in 1763 and fought against the British in 1768 and in the Anglo-Nepal war of 1814–16. The British were so impressed with the bravery of the Gurkhas that they recruited them into the British Army. They played a decisive role in the Indian mutiny of 1875. More than 114,000 Gurkhas fought in the First World War. In the Second World War their numbers expanded to 45 battalions. Today, Gurkha troops are still recruited from Nepal and sent to Hong Kong for training. In Nepal Gurkhas are held in high esteem and are also important earners of foreign exchange bringing in about US$15 million a year — second only to the income from tourism.

H _____

Highest point Mount Everest, also known as Sagarmatha in Nepal and Qomolangma in Tibet. At 8,848 m (29,028 ft) it is the highest point on earth.

I _____

Indrajatra The most spectacular annual Nepali festival, lasting eight days and celebrated by both Hindus and Buddhists. The festival is held at the end of the rainy season to honour the god Indra who rules rain and prosperity.

J _____

Jhankris The shamans of the Tamang people. Shamanism is a feature of many Nepali people's lives as well as devotion to Buddhism and Hinduism. Jhankris are employed to conduct religious ceremonies such as driving out spirits and performing seasonal agricultural rites. Their shamanic rites are similar to those found amongst the Mongolian and Siberian people, from whom many Nepalis are descended.

K _____

Kalo Bhairab A huge stone image in Durbar Square, Kathmandu which was once used as a form of lie detector. Telling lies in front of the statue was believed to bring instant death.

King of Nepal Nepal is a Hindu country ruled by the only Hindu monarch in the world. The autonomy of the kingdom was established by King Manadeva (462–505). The reigning monarch is His Majesty King Birendra Bir Bikram Shah Dev. He is regarded as an avatar (reincarnation) of Vishnu, the preserver, one of the principal Hindu deities.

Kumari In the Kathmandu Valley lives the Kumari or Living Goddess. The Kumari is a young girl chosen from a caste of Newari goldsmiths. She is usually chosen when she is five years old and must never have been hurt or shed blood. There are usually about 10 candidates who are selected by several people including an astrologer. The candidates are locked in a dark room where terrifying masks and freshly killed buffalo heads are kept. The girl who shows the least fear is selected. The Kumari lives in a three-storied building — the Kumari Devi — until she reaches puberty. Once a year, in September, she is paraded around the streets of Kathmandu and taken to see the King whom she blesses.

L _____

Languages .There are 36 languages spoken in Nepal. 58% speak Nepali; 3% speak Newari (mainly in Kathmandu); 20% speak Indian languages; the rest speak various dialects.

Life expectancy Average life expectancy is 44 years for males and 47 years for females. Old age is venerated and when an old person reaches the auspicious age of 77 years, seven months and seven days the pasni ceremony is performed. This is the same ceremony as that performed when babies are seven months old.

Location The Kingdom of Nepal lies at the centre of the great arc of the Himalaya between Tibet in the north and India in the south.

M _____

Mahadevi The most important female deity in Nepal. In Hinduism she is the Great Goddess, also called Parvati, the consort of Shiva. She has many names and incarnations, the most fearful of which is the black goddess Kali. In this aspect the goddess has an insatiable greed for blood of demons, animals and human beings. All over Nepal many rites in honour of her involve the sacrifice of animals, which must always be male. Until 1780, when it was officially banned, these rituals also included human sacrifices.

Mahayana Buddhism A major school of Buddhism which now predominates in Nepal. One of the central beliefs of Mahayana Buddhism is that one can obtain nirvana by following bodhisattvas (Buddhas-to-be). These bodhisattvas are enlightened beings who have reincarnated to help others attain enlightenment.

Malla Dynasty One of the most remarkable kings of Nepal, Jayasthiti Malla (1380–1422) reigned for 53 years. Trade routes over the central Himalaya were established, creating intricate economic and commercial patterns. Jayasthiti's grandson Yaksha Malla (1428–82) divided the kingdom amongst his heirs. The division created a long period of interstate rivalry but also a period of great cultural activity. The Malla dynasty lasted 400 years until 1767.

Muktinath A holy place at Pokhara where a natural gas flame and water issue from the same rock.

N

Newars The original inhabitants of the Kathmandu Valley, they still have a distinct identity and language. Nepali culture is heavily influenced by the art and literature of the Newars, especially their woodcarving which is highly prized. The traditional Newari style of architecture includes the brick built temple with diminishing tiered roofs. Historians now believe this style originated in ancient India, where it was subsequently abandoned. It has become the hallmark of Nepali architecture.

P

Pashupati A Hindu deity unique to Nepal, Pashupati is an aspect of Shiva and is the protector of animals and of the Kathmandu Valley.

Pokhara A small town 200 km (124 mi) west of Kathmandu, Pokhara is a favourite destination for travellers in Nepal. It is virtually in the geographical centre of Nepal and lies beneath the Annapurna range of mountains. 20 years ago it was a small hamlet where even the primitive bullock cart was unknown until introduced by aeroplane in 1961. Today the town has a population of some 50,000 people. Local legend has it that Phewa Lake, which lies beside the town, covers an ancient settlement which was flooded by water released by an earthquake.

Population About 17 million with some 42% under the age of 15.

Proselytism Converting another to one's own faith is forbidden by law in Nepal and those attempting to proselytize can face lengthy jail sentences. This reflects the tradition of religious tolerance in Nepal.

Puja The ritual offerings made at shrines every morning by most Nepalis.

R

Rato Machhendra Machhendra is the popular Tantric god of rain and plenty. He is also worshipped by the Hindus as an incarnation of Shiva. The red (rato) Machhendra is a representation of the god made from red wood which is paraded around the streets of Patan in a chariot every year in May. Every 12 years the chariot is pulled to Bungamati which is 5 km (3 mi) away. Rato Machhendra has a second residence in Bungamati where he spends six months of every year.

Religion Officially, 90% of the people are Hindus, 8% are Buddhists and 2% are Islamic. However, Hinduism and Buddhism overlap with devotees of both worshipping at each other's shrines.

S

Shah, Prithvi Narayan The Shah unified the country in 1769 with the approval of the British East India Company which had backed his claim to sovereignty. This ended the divisions of the 400-year Malla dynasty.

T

Tantrism The Tantrist cult influences both Buddhism and Hinduism in Nepal. The word tantra is an analogy to the weft and the warp of weaving, expressing the interrelatedness of everything in life. The numerous Tantric deities are usually multiple-limbed. A tantra is a religious script which contains a magic formula.

Terrain 14% of the land is cultivated, 13% is pasture, 32% is forested, the rest is heavily mountainous.

V

Vaisha Dev The toothache god whose image is situated in Kathmandu and who gives relief for toothache when a nail or coin is hammered into the ground in front of him.

Y

Yab-yum A Tibetan concept which has been integrated into Nepali art. Yab-yum is similar to the Chinese concept of yin-yang. It expresses the male and female qualities which appear in Nepali art through the painting and sculpting of couples such as Shiva-Pavarti.

Z

Zone of Peace King Birendra's proposal to turn Nepal into an internationally recognized 'Zone of Peace' has been endorsed by 80 countries including China.

INDEX